Playing for Time

Jane Spiro

For dear Jean
a ray of sunshine —
may you at last have time
for everyone and everything
you love,
warm wishes,
Jane Spiro

Oversteps Books

First published in 2015 by   Oversteps Books Ltd
                               6 Halwell House
                               South Pool
                               Nr Kingsbridge
                               Devon
                               TQ7 2RX
                               UK

www.overstepsbooks.com

Copyright © 2015 Jane Spiro
ISBN 978-1-906856-57-1

All rights reserved. No part of this book may be reproduced, stored in a retrieval system, or transmitted in any form, or by any means, electronic, mechanical, photocopying, recording or otherwise, or translated into any language, without prior written permission from Oversteps Books, except by a reviewer who may quote brief passages in a review.

The right of Jane Spiro to be identified as the author of this work has been asserted by her in accordance with the Copyright, Designs and Patents Act 1988.

Printed in Great Britain by imprint digital, Devon

*for John
and for the Spiros, Ostermans, Seymours and Daniels,
the water in which I swim*

Acknowledgements

With thanks to the editors of the following magazines and anthologies in which some of these poems have appeared:
Rialto, The Journal, Resurgence, North Stone Review; South West Arts, Peterloo, Kent and Sussex, Oxfordshire Love and Justice prizewinner collections;
Confluence (Two Rivers), Moor Poets 3, East of Auden, Children at War, Eating your Cake and Having it (Fatchance Press), Poetry as a Foreign Language (White Adder Press) Uncharted (Moor Poets) and Oxford Poetry on the Buses; three poetry-photo exhibitions at the Ariel Centre in Totnes with John Daniel and Michael Carter: Written in Stone, Marking the Land, and Watermarks.

Poems in this collection have benefited from the critical friendship of Weir Poets, Two Rivers, Back Room Poets, Stanza Two, Moor Poets, Plymouth Poetry Exchange, Treacle Wellingtons and Rewley House classes.

But most of all thanks and indebtedness are due to my partner and co-creator in life and in poetry, John Daniel.

Contents

Part 1: Where to Look
As a solstice gift   1
Where to look   2
From stone to flesh   3
Netsuke   4
Totnes Castle   5
clapper bridge   6
Cloistered   7
Mission house mirror, Hawai'i   8
Hawai'ian gathering   9
Wild flowers elegy   10
Company of cows   11
Deer struck   12
A place for washing clean   13
Seaside signs   14
The new machine   15
Twelve ways to smile   16

Part 2: Changing Shoes
Changing shoes   17
Lost, found   18
Hallsands abandoned   19
nothing I touch stands still   20
A la ronde   21
The Inner Tango   22
Dante's goddess   23
Curfew   24
Forced evacuation in black and white   25
The wake   26
Portrait of a Madman   27
Redundant   28
Snow work   29
Bastille day   30
The shoe-shiner   31
Kindness   32

Part 3: Teaching us Time

Bearded lizard	33
Mesmerised by bells	34
Man and machine	35
Meeting rhino	36
Free horse	37
Maria's dog	38
Learning to walk	39
Children's pictures, Theriesenstadt	40
Mother/Clock	42
Playing for time	43
Return to the first language	44
Forbidden city	45
Grandfather cut glass	46
Moments Musicaux	48
for the surgeon: when my dad was tiny	49
Violin romance	50
Here is that song	51

As a solstice gift

                I give you
three people you love –
one very young with new-down hair,
one very old with a face lived many times,
one in its prime with ripe-berry skin.

As a solstice gift I will open a door,
a window, a curtain for you
and behind, beyond, inside
will be something you have just seen
for the first time.

As a solstice gift I give you
a special time for gifts,
the special gift you have already,
or could have, with a leap, a small leap,
yours or mine.

Where to look

This museum is a not-museum
where things of no interest
are collected meticulously together in glass cases
labelled with no information
and forming a story of no coherence –

a tired saint rimmed with flaking gold
propped against a door,
portrait of an unknown nobody smiling
for no particular reason, a dusty sedan chair,
a bottle shaped as a clown, a room
of stuffed birds shocked to be there –

but the floor is magnificent.
Yes, I would be here, amazed,
for the floor alone.
My feet are threaded on a spider's web,
a fretted chessboard of light and dark.

The planet is here.
Look under your feet.

From stone to flesh
Ermington Church, South Devon

Nearby is a church with a twist
in its spire – it turned to greet the beauty
of a local bride, and was frozen
in its tracks for the sin of desire.

So goes the myth.

Inside the church is the wooden pulpit
carved by Violet, daughter of the vicar,
her ring of saints in wooden gowns,
their hands carved flat into their chests
or holding books or babies,
or pointing skywards –

all but one, who stretches out his hands
in walnut sleeves, inviting you to hold them
in yours, and when you do
you can feel how the wood has smoothed to a polish
and the fingers have been stroked to a blur,
still warm as if they have danced around a maypole
on a hot village afternoon, or been circled
in the palm of a parish child longing to grow up.

So stories go, leaping from stone to wood to flesh.

Netsuke

How it was the smallest space between
being and not being, sitting on its double,
paw to paw on the antique shop mirror.

How it turned in that second, sensing
the scuttle of a distant mouse, and you
made it again, that sudden feral spark,

shaved tiny skins of wood, smoothed
its back, its walnut tail taut with life,
paw transmuting from soft to barbed,

signed your name in *kanji* between the claws,
marking your place, your spot of time
made into shape before it fled.

Totnes Castle

From the ground we seem to have grown
without cause or pattern, any-old-how,
walls, high windows, ancient airborne trees,
a scrum, a scattering, an accident of life.

The Normans knew this, flew to the tops
of hills, built castles, played gods
looking down on the shape of things,
the narrow-facing nests of roofs,

saw the cobweb plans of our lanes,
the inevitableness of our comings and
goings, the way the view from the hill
made of us tiny strutting dolls –

the way things are in sleep
when we become a bird,
fly over the landscape of our own life.

clapper bridge

How many men must have hauled
this huge flag of stone
from its calf-bed to the rift
in the earth where the river
crazed and broke ground,
sheep-shearer, hunter, herdsman,
how they hoisted the mono-lith
on to rope-taut shoulders and
laid it stone-cold across the flood,
their burden-gift, offering that day,
how we can hear them now
in the chatter of the clapper bridge,
spread under our step
a hundred lifetimes away.

Cloistered

Suddenly finding ourselves at dusk
in cloisters, names of war-lost youths
melded into stone, shadows
where no-one lingers,

a stone face falls open
and white-robed choristers process out,
glow-worms lit by candles,
floating in the strangeness of dark,
chanting *kyries*.

We watch as if uncovering,
in the heart of an unexpected cave,
a coven of secret moths
spreading paper wings,
thinking they are alone –

a shadow life where the dead
have carried on living
though we failed to see them –
ghostly-light in the white of day.

Mission house mirror, Hawaii

The missionaries taught not only

how shapes were words
but how it was

to stare at oneself as a stranger might
and see your eyes, crossed with surprise,
face fixed and frozen,
staring at yourself staring at yourself,
floating like spirits, on the other side,
in a parallel room,
looking through a window through a wall
and seeing the inside from the outside

so when they knocked on the missionary door
and heard
    Have you come in search of God, my child?
they said
    oh no, miss, could we look in the mirror?

Hawaiian gathering

Squatting limber among the leaves
you could tell from the taut of his neck
how well he knew his task,
choosing from the library of the earth

>*black nightshade   torch ginger*
>*mountain apple   air yarn*
>*Indian shot amaumau fern*

the list of the edible,
he sorted them, fast from feast from poison,
surely as a bird might search,
plucked them briskly from their stem,

>*kukui   liliko'i*
>*pink wood   ohelo ai*
>*sea grape lilac tasselflower*

reader of a dying code, he searched
the braille of their delicate veins
slowly as if the earth had time, and
finding them, bowed head to head,
thanking them for their sacrifice.

>*Aloha i ka wai niu o ka aina*
>Oh loved land of new wine of the palm.

Wild flowers elegy
extinct and endangered Dartmoor flowers

broad buckler-fern   moonwort
southern marsh orchid
moon daisy

> *oh waly waly bedlam*
> *cold blows the wind-oh*

black knapweed marsh thistle
common cat's-ear
autumn hawk-bit   rough hawk-bit

> *oh waly waly bedlam*
> *cold blows the wind-oh*

devil's-bit scabious
common mouse-ear   chickweed
sheep's sorrel   self-heal

> *oh waly waly bedlam*
> *cold blows the wind-oh*

hay rattle   eyebright
birdsfoot trefoil
field forget-me-not

> *oh waly waly bedlam*
> *cold blows the wind-oh*

Company of cows

They stand as if alone
in the primal light of that early field,
caught suddenly in company,

their tails long, heavy pendulums,
large buttock bones clumped together,
heads hidden in the heat of the circle –

no champing at a trough
or at clumps of graze grass, no brushing or scrambling,
but standing in each other's body warmth

making a dry patch amongst fields
blotted with winter inks, a quiet scrum
against the pool-cold world.

Deer struck

Suddenly it apparitioned in from darkness,
its russet brush-back clear as touch,
and we were locked in the brightness,
each hair clear strikes of diagonal rain

and I could see the leanness of your
nearly-grown body in the split second
my own movement, unstoppable,
ploughed into your warm animal thigh,

alien, unfair metal
invading the forest in your head,
my sprint for freedom downing yours,
your machine for living cut short by mine.

A place for washing clean
Roman wash-house, Cefalù, Sicily

They wash feet here
down in the damp stone below the street
where the water runs along sluices
unsettling the dust from crusty pores,
cool runnels, unstoppable.

We do not know who we are meant to be
but our feet do, the water does –
Greek, Roman, Arab, Turkish, Portuguese –
a thousand years of washing,
unwrapping the layers of city cloy,
the colours of skin, joining us all
in its rush back to earth.

Seaside signs
Cornish coastal path

There will be no feeding of seagulls,
making of picnic noises, eating of ice cream
by children, dogs, or other.

There must be no leaving of litter,
lipstick, lovenests, shells, shingle. Dunes
must be collected before departure.
This water is not for drinking, swimming,
activity of fish that may cause offence.

If in distress contact the coastguard HQ
in Southampton, the freefone on the Devon freeway
junction 18, the lighthouse centre in London,
the rubber ring heart defibrilllator
at the primary care centre in Caerphilly.

This Tor was donated by
this cliff was bought by
this wind, this air, this cloud,
this cowslip, this cow
was the generous gift of
the Duke, Earl, Prince, Lady,
to the people of Cornwall.

Only enter sandcastles with hard hats.
The sea is closed
for vital repairs.

The new machine
Kilmainham jail, Dublin 1868

Until the camera caught them staring into the lens,
eyes schooled to conceal the soul,
cheek and nose doubled in the side mirror,
hands with fingers spread over chest to reveal
the oddities of thumb and joints –

until then it was possible to disappear,
wipe your record clear, slide a name in and out of sight.
You could arrive, stolen goods trailing behind you –
a purple rooster, barnbrack, a pocked potato –

and then erase yourself, melt back into the city,
become born again – Kathleen, poacher and prostitute,
Padraig boatbuilder, Mikie shoemaker,
Vince carpenter, Molly seamstress –

but now this black box pins them with its greedy eye,
fixes them unsmiling in the wooden chair,
pulls their image from the mix of light and shade,
pastes them down so it is a face you can never escape,
a black and white from which there is no running.

Twelve ways to smile
found from lessons in Thai *by Map and Hamish Chalmers*

the 'I'm so happy I'm crying' smile:
    yim thang nam taa
the 'polite' smile for someone you barely know:
    yim thak thaai
the 'I admire you' smile:
    yim cheun chom
the stiff smile, also known as the
 'I should laugh at the joke though it's not funny' smile:
    fuen yim
the smile which masks something wicked in your mind:
    yim mee lessanai
the teasing or 'I told you so' smile:
    yim yaw
the 'I know things look pretty bad but there's no point in
        crying over spilt milk' smile:
    yim yae-yae
the dry smile, also known as the 'I know I owe you the money but I don't have it' smile:
    yim haeng
the 'I disagree with you' smile, also known as the 'You can go ahead and propose it but your idea's no good' smile:
    yim thak thaan
the 'I am the winner' smile, given to the loser:
    yim cheua-cheuan
the 'smiling in the face of an impossible struggle' smile:
    yim soo
the 'I'm trying to smile but can't' smile:
    yim mai awk

Changing shoes

Our mothers matched us at six
at the corner shop.

We were suitable girls
to eat sponge cake, ride bicycles

and when we met again
it all came back, the years,

the stories, laid back to back
like sardines, between bus stops.

My shoes were red like strawberries
squashed at the end of summer,

hers were blue-black, two large leeches
mis-shapen from over-lunching –

hers pinched, mine sprawled
so we swapped shoes.

For a long slice of road
we spread toes in new moulds

and I wore her chemist shop,
two brothers, Dutchman,
caves and singing lessons

and she wore my lilac tree,
goatskin drum, calypso singer
and broken engagements.

Lost, found
Shipwrecks in Salcome bay, South Devon

and when we went there the sand was strewn
with lumps of soap, waxy, rough on the skin –
how I hated it, but it was free,
the sea had issued it up.
         Louis Sheid   1939, South Milton beach

and when we went there the brig had gone down,
the wine barrels in their hundreds broken up
and the sea, claret-coloured it was, mixed with salt,
not a drop for us to drink, the sea took it all.
         Unidentified   French brig 1869

it was the gale that did for him, that,
and that he lay in the arms of his bride
below deck, to live, to die, waiting
for the sea to choose.
         Gossamer   1868 Prawle Point

Hallsands abandoned
The village of Hallsands slid into the sea on January 27th 1917

How it stands now, ghost of itself,
sea invading its spaces, houses –
their hearts eaten by waves,
open to the wild of wind. How nature

drives all before it, fishermen
who abandoned nets, children
who kept guard on clifftops
as the sea turned mad, the post mistress

sealing her last stamp, the pigs
shooed squealing from their piggery,
the last sacrament of the chapel
closing its Bible doors, and the children

straggling on their two-mile walk to school
that day of no return –
how it must have been, walking out
with the coals still warm, the chimneys

still surprised with smoke, the fireplace
where the child saved from drowning
was laid down, wrapped in blankets –

cold now, all of them, gone, and cold.

nothing I touch stands still
Katherine Carver from Doncaster sailed from Plymouth to New England in the Mayflower   September 1620

We held with our eyes to the edge –
held until spread England
slipped away, not knowing where to,
forgetting where from –

the colour of waves read me,
red for climbing high, feeling fire,
yellow for fear and turning sick,
white for my father's beard, dales in frost,
gold for the new-found-land
and for my marriage band –

the ground is bewitched into water –
nowhere to root – spread – plant –
are we winged?

There is no end between wave and cloud
and the sun has fallen in ribbons
under our feet,
the sky sliced below us, its face
a dragon's back, all its anger dark,

and nothing I touch
stands still.

A la ronde

A La Ronde was built in 1795 by two spinster cousins who bequeathed the house in perpetuity to unmarried kinswomen.

I never wanted to pose with a fan of baby boys
or dandle on the end of a merchant's wrist
dropping grain for the family tree

nor did it suit to sew samplers,
tracing the routes of straying suitors
with silver finger nails on the parlour globe.

Not for me to freeze in still portraits,
a pink spouse with pedicured spaniel,
to print the name of sons
on the patriarchal tomb and title deeds.

I am the one who sat unladylike on donkeys,
washed shells in the bath tub, pressed feathers
into the walls and spun globes of the world like baubles.

I am the daughter who burst from the family tree
as a single bud, bloomed and fruited
from the tree with no name but my own.

Here is my stone dropped in a pool panning out
rings within rings of generations:
 for all pools spread with a single stone
 for all those who gather shells
 for all daughters with one name.

The Inner Tango

The woman at the next table
loves her shoes.

She does not think about
the selves above the table
who live their lives soberly
in service to her needs.

No, her mind is under the table
where it has spilt *va va voom*
into her red shoes,
is having a glorious fling
with danger.

Suspended on a stiletto,
spiked and chilli hot, it cavorts
with itself, circling the air
with a glint of buckle silver,
clinging by a single strap
to its secret dance
under the table,

dancing her other self,
her inner tango.

Dante's goddess

Beatrice was 8 when Dante first met her. They met only once more in her lifetime, and they never spoke. She was the subject of his greatest poems. She died aged 24 from the plague.

Before I was a goddess I was a girl
carrying fish from market in baskets.

I wanted to drink wine with loud men,
and walk through town at night
when boys became dangerous,
know their secret talk,

to learn, slowly, how it would be
to wear velvet and ivory at my throat.

But then I became your goddess,
more than my black curls pulled into summer caps,
more than my bodice cut so tight I cried,
more than the way wine would make me
laugh, more than all these
did you make me, more than myself.

I believed it, frozen into that moment of life
where you liked me, a smiling icon
pressed flat by your dreams –

you pressed the breath from me,
stole the wind in my veil,
painted my bloom flat
in the leaves of your book –

when I felt the dark flower
open out in my blood
you gave me metaphors.

It was not more than myself
you loved, not myself
at all.

Curfew
Kashmir 1984

On land ankle chains and skull caps bake
on tin trays, pipefires from hookahs
and mint tea steam

> *the clip of poles in thick water,*
> *the rind of peeled fruit*

as the crack of mainland guns collect
like the sough of mosquitoes after monsoon.
Curfew creeps up like dark cats.
We hardly know its scratch.

The ladies used to sit here
under parasols in white cottons
sampling the summer winds
rolled from the Indus rocks to the lake,
pressing orchid petals, washing their hair
in jasmine, drinking tea with ghee

here, where we sit. The little girl floats by,
her hair strung with flowers –
she slews through lotus flats
selling marigold garlands and bags of henna,
painted boxes, mangos cut like clowns' lips,

as night drops down, tight as an outgrown bangle.
We didn't notice nightfall either,
when the first man cut curfew.

He was walking home late
when guncracks threw him
where donkey pats drew flies
and the dust dragged red
and his cap, once white as sabre teeth,
was kicked under a cow's hoof,
and never retrieved .

Forced evacuation in black and white

Slapton Sands was evacuated by the Admiralty for naval exercises during the Second World War. Many of the villagers were forced to give up farming livelihoods and never returned to their homes.

The woman stands at the closed door
as if fixed, or longing to be fixed,
her felt black hat with wide brim,
best winter coat buttoned for last warmth.

The film's grain cracks her moves
into puppet-clicks, as she walks woodenly
down the garden path,
its spring display muted to grey.

She knows the leaving is for
a greater good, the disappearing of all
over the edge of the sea,
> *helmets washed back to beach
> rusted and pitted with hidden fire.*

The army truck waits in the road,
table legs strung up like a slaughtered cow,
squeezed elbows of armchairs disgraced,
upended, unclothed –

she jigs to the gate and back again,
to and fro between the two,
the door, the gate, the gate, the door,
denying the shock of the truck,
its skill for taking away –

betrayed, commits the final breach –
steps into the road, stops,
turns back

frozen in the film's frame,
the last look letting go of all.

The wake
*Cesseras, Languedoc, region of the Cathars, early dissenters
massacred by the Crusaders after 1208*

The lady was very old, they said, over eighty,
for many years not of this world.
That's her house opposite the church,
the shutters closed, the dust
gathering. She has seen
the vineyards ripen, the bells
ringing out the hours.

The lady was very old, they said, over ninety,
her mind no longer of this world.
That's her house in the tower. She saw
German tanks block the narrow lanes,
remembers when her language
was a crime. She has seen
the vineyards go to seed, the bells
ringing out the hours.

The lady was very old, they said, centuries old,
her memories too strong for living.
That's her house with windows slitted
like strongholds, hiding places.
She knew what it was to be a lost tribe,
to watch the fountains gasping
for air. She has seen the land
starved of seed, known the bells
ringing out the hours.

That's her resting place, in the box
spread with white roses. These
are her people, filling the village church,
chanting their dirge. But she –

she has known the bells
ringing out the hours –
pe pe   pe pe   pe pe
    dong   dong   dong
hear my tongue,
    I have seen,
        I have been.

Portrait of a Madman
by Géricault

Each page turn in my book of art
shook out fairground colours,
a holiday umbrella or olive grove

but when I folded you out,
your limp gown clung to the scooped wings
of your neck and your hair
stood up in black tufts, uncombed,
shocked like fire.

It was not that, not the empty loop
of your palm, holding nothing,
that held me then, but the blue waste of your eyes
where a hell was fixed, cut into your mask
like broken snow.

You were a scene of abandoned children
screened into my page, lifting a finger
from your cold century, pasting your blood
in brown paint on mine.

They labelled you 'Madman'
to remind me you were not numbered
amongst the Tuscan dukes, Holbein's merchants
in soft caps, bearded apostles.

They label you under underground bridges
with men in tinfoil and dustbin bags,
acid house fallouts and station drunks

but in my book, your absent hand
bores a tunnel in the page
and your eyes tell me of their winter

and my hand is frozen
in the act of turning.

Redundant

I am returning the enclosed.

It is
too long too short too big
too small too tight too loose

the wrong colour
shape   size   cut
texture fabric fit

disliked by my
lover   daughter   neighbour
dean   doctor   dog
dentist   psychic counsellor.

It is used   soiled   surplus to requirements
unsatisfactory   no longer required
unfortunately redundant.

You have signed an agreement
that you will accept your status
without complaint.

Terms and conditions are non-reversible.

Dispose of quietly
after use

Snow work

The snow has grounded the workers
and only snow-work snow-play
is to be done today.

The neighbour has ditched his dawn start
and instead shovels the white dune of his
doorstep into a dump on the open drive,
builds it load by load into a lolling
giant anthill half his height.

Now he squats before the ghost
he has made, his mittened paws patting
and shaping, freeing soft flakes of quartz
on to his damp sleeve, summoning the white
space into form with his hands,

then stands to view his work, complete,
a smiling moon face with pudding cheeks,
pool-pebble eyes and deep drawn grin,
bundled warm inside a loosely knotted scarf,
plump and rooted to his ground.

Another kind of work was done today,
another kind of getting-things-done,
built like the seasons, to come and go,
built because the moment told him so.

Bastille day

The Moroccan family restaurant
has spread its tables across the street
under the awnings, on towards
the promenade, the sea.

The concierge in her batik dress
numbers the tables with sticky labels,
arranges napkins in fans on plates,
still calm, in control,

but the guests are unstoppable, they flock in
like starlings migrating to Africa, cloning
tables to the far horizon. Harassed brothers
in white aprons appear from the doorway,

the father who never intended to join in, sweating
under his trays, the ten-year old daughter
with chubby knees running between the rows
holding wine glasses by the stem

and then, resentfully plucked from her planet,
the teenage daughter in tight white jeans
teetering on heels, balancing tagines
on her elbows, they weave in and out,

the family with all its branches blossoming
and the eaters, snatching at the menus,
chattering, complaining, spilling wine
until, at last, when the hour has come,

the mama appears, fierce as a mantis
in black lace juggling her couscous
as the dark spills over the ocean and coloured fire
bursts against the pitch screen of sky.

The shoe-shiner
Granada in summer

The shoe-shiner carries his shining in a magic box
with sliding panels that open out into brushes.
He ballets his chamois leather from hand to hand,
his polishes in coloured pats –

flits from one secret compartment to another,
quick as a flea, seesaws my shoes
with brushes and leathers until their faces,
rubbed and pinched, squeak like mice.

Like new! he says, and is as pleased as I am.
I point my toes, walk squeaking,
down the street.

This he knows, my shoe-shiner,
conjurer against the dust and tumble.
He makes illusion from the magic box.

It makes new,
        and what he does passes by,
        and what he does passes by.

Kindness

In the narrow lane between beach and road
a man is lying propped up against the wall,
groaning,

and in the dark two others bend over,
cradling his shoulders, murmuring
viens viens

as he flops forward in their arms,
a grounded fish, *je ne marche pas*
he says, *I can't walk.*

They enfold him, slung like a limp catch
between their shoulders, whispering
doucement doucement,

walking him back to the patch of land
where he beaches, waiting for daylight
to dry him.

That, and kindness, was all he needed.

Bearded lizard

Arms akimbo hold him
blended to branch, muscles chubbed,
dressed in stitched grids of skin –

he lifts the blind
of his hooded eye, turns inside the
layered walnut of his head,

waits for hunger to become worm,
cricket make sound, become food,
reptile rise up *homo erectus* –

time machine, holding millennia
in his five-fingered hand, teaching us time –
how it cannot be counted.

Mesmerised by bells

Because the sounds would not let me leave
I find a bench to sit amongst them, mesmerised,
when an old man, shuffling between son and wife,
stops, caught by the bells, the spell

> *bluebells*
> *light up early grass*

Take my seat, I say
and we both, compelled somehow to do so,
bow to one another

> *the river finds its course,*
> *runs to quiet sea*

Man and machine

When the iron gate creaks open
here is a man with a spade
and another, then another,
to supervise the removal of the gravel.

They sit along the wall,
under the walnut tree, in the shade.

Then it arrives, rattling
and snorting through the gate,
its giant scoop jointed and
clanking like a flapping jaw.

The three men coax and harry it
to its place, holding their spades.

Puffing and grating, its iron haunches
cranked into place, it bobs down,
once, twice, thrice,
grinding the hot dust in its metal teeth,
choking and spitting on its rocky porridge
until the driveway is clean.

The men sit on the wall in a line,
spades at rest, under the walnut tree,

contemplate their limits, their machine.

Meeting rhino

Baboon on a bench
scratches its head with a forefinger,
pink nails, frill of fur,

and we are not so different –
puzzled, pink,
finding furniture in forests

when slate-grey shambles into focus,
legs flapping, loose leather,
it moves as if carrying its battle tent

painfully about it, ageing armour
useless, the last warrior
in a history book of myths and unicorns.

All its friends are stories,
trophies, drinking horns.
Elder of a lost tribe,

its eyes pin us
in their weary victory,
and finding of us nothing,

it turns, trailing leather heels
puttputt puttputt behind,
slow bottom melting into bush,

as we gape, little people
in our metal tank,
voyeurs from a guilty planet

Free horse
Grand National

They were running in a pack,
thundering over jumps
in chase one of another,
ankle to ankle to dust
to breath

when one shook off its rider
and ran regardless,
driven by the gun of its passion,
the sweat on the skin of its rivals,
the taut snare of its aim

and I know how it is
riderless to run for the lost goal,
skirting the hurdle others jumped
on to your own finish
your own lone win.

Maria's dog

This is the dog's driveway
and the driveway is for the dog.

The dog lies in his driveway
and the shade from the two gates
meets in the middle of his back
and washes around his paws.

The car is orange and wishes to depart
through the gates which are for the dog.

The car stops. It seems agitated.
This is strange, as the dog, whose gates it is,
is not at all agitated.

The car bristles and swells like a bee,
its shiny nose nudges the dog
out of his shade, drives away.

The dog watches the car as it drives away.

Then he moves into the driveway.

This is the dog's driveway
and the driveway is for the dog.

Learning to walk
for Emily

How the world is for the first time
possible to navigate, how it is
a room to cross, from prop to prop

learning speed, how to make it –
the shock of a sudden hurt or this
a soft fall into giving sand

and you never know until you tumble
which it will be, and there's a kind of bliss
in the testing of floors –

in seeing how it is when the running stops,
cut short by ground, not sure which it is,
ground leaping up, or you reaching down

and when the solid takes you by surprise,
as if forever, there are hands –
sudden hands that lift you up.

Children's pictures, Theresienstadt

First they painted memories of home,
neat garden paths, houses with open doors,
mothers in aprons, sisters dressing dolls,
families lit with candles on Friday night
happy at table, plaited bread, braided cloth,
faces with crayon smiles and curls, brothers.

Then they painted stories, changeling brothers,
prince and pauper, fairy princess at home
in castles or caves, trees with secret doors,
three bears with bowls at table, wooden dolls
that grow long noses, pied piper at night
leading children away, knights with gold cloth.

Then they painted the leaving, packing clothes
candlesticks, leaving cats, toys, books, brothers,
stick men walking with the remnants of home
in square cases, labelled, trains with barred doors
moving on pencil rails, people drawn like dolls,
heads in the windows, sky scribbled out, night.

Then they painted the room where, day and night
they lived, slept – bunk beds, striped clothes,
barren table, bare walls, shaven heads, no brothers,
fathers, mothers, a new denuded home,
walls without windows, exits without doors,
no candlesticks, no cats, no games, no dolls.

Then they drew the gallows, broken dolls
hanging, guns spraying pencil shot, night
raids of black scribbled bombs, stick-people, clothes
ragged, spattered, people running, friends, brothers
stooped, splayed against fences, nightmare of home
on fire, faces in flames, seen through open doors.

Then they painted going home, through the door
to silver woods, ochre farms, clutching dolls
and suitcases on empty roads, midnight
moons lighting paths, fields laid like golden cloth,
magic carpets back to mothers, brothers,
signposts to Prague, Josefov, Široká street, home.

Then absence, doors to nowhere, moonless night,
an end of dolls, brothers, Sabbath cloth, home –
these images remaining and us, their witness.

Mother/Clock

I can tell the time by your face.

At dawn you are seen
through a firstborn haze
as the landing stage,
the first and only port.

In the morning you fill still
my little space as I try
to make it grow,
test what I know.

At noon I tear
from you, kick you away,
set my own pace,
paint my own face.

In early afternoon
I am on a highpoint of time,
balancing all the loads of life,
forgetting yours, obsessed with mine.

In late afternoon I see
what I did not want to know –
that for all the distance
I thought I'd gone

it was your face all along.

Playing for time

For Bar Mitvah the family clubbed together
to buy a piano, one of his own
to scale mazurkas, rondos, nocturnes,
the courts of Esterházy, Polish drinking houses,
bordellos and ballrooms, revolutionary sonatas,
sunken cathedrals, songs without words.

It rocked from sea edge to edge,
bore its burden-voyage, jaws closed
in the damp ship bowels

to the cold north, new neighbours,
sealed doorways, languages
without words, unsung home.

Its voluptuous curves, shining smile,
banged against walls, outswept arms
clawed the bony bars of banisters,
punched at closed windows

and then, its hungry ivory gnashing at air,
was demoted to the street, shuffled out,
a failure to fit.

We learn not to long for
things, to forget them
since they forget us –

not to long for
places we once sang,
spread under our hands,
felled with hammers.

Return to the first language

I first heard my nursery language
on some freezing platform,
dockland choking up a sunless dawn.

This is the land where sepia children
with soil black tresses, grew into long breeches,
leather satchels, the long walk to school.

Yet these are no more my roots
than a bird claiming a branch
that has broken.
We were blown like pollen,
each place of landing a place to spring,
laying roots where the wind ended,
where it let us rest –

wrote out inventions to quiet the past,
tried for home wherever we fell,
where the double boots for deep frost
and prayer books were unpacked,
where the cheesecake baked again.

I am not of this place
where I hear from the dockland workers
language stolen from nursery rhymes,
from half-remembered stories, prayers
that found new tongues, started again.

Forbidden city
Warsaw 1938; Warsaw 1998

You remember the childhood city
where you skated in the winter park,
the schoolbag passed from brother to brother,
the rules of where to go

and not to go – the coffee houses,
cathedral square, university gates,
the way they were not yours to know.

Since then your heart has opened,
the city has grown a face of stone –
House of Culture, concreted park,
grids of apartment blocks, cloned shop fronts,
town square where tourist horses
toss braided manes.

the ice rink was here you say, by the Burger King doorway,
and our apartment
paved over now with names of Russian heroes
and the synagogue – somewhere here
as if the earth has a memory.

The journey is to find the places
you never knew, your forbidden city.
I want to see the University, you say.

You stand there now, tiny, white-haired, free,
and look through the iron gates
down to the shadowy, snarling open door.

Grandfather cut glass

Because there was danger in broken glass,
the way light was bottle-green, the way your hands
were nicked with glass-cuts, stained yellow,
the jaunt of your black fedora, and the always-ash
dripping from your lip, glass was the thing that was
you. The kingfisher blues, oil-yellows, the reds

like crushed raspberries, the bloodclot reds
and all the shapes, roses, trees of life, glass
rainbows, house numbers, all the thing that was
you blossomed on suburban doors, your hands
making entrances, streets of them, your dripping-ash
hands, your grandfather hands, your hands stained yellow –

light refracted through glass, blue-red-yellow
partly-seen children, corridors through whirlpool reds
in kaleidoscope whorls, number sixes with ash,
silver putty edges, spaniel faces in blue-glow through glass
all made by you, your large hands
that held ice-creams. In the back seat I was

small amongst broken glass, the thing that was
you, sitting amongst the jigsaw-edges, the parrot yellow
and princess blue, holding them in my hands
like small fish, sliding, slippery, see-through reds,
the car-smell of oil, the bright-light glass,
the way you growled gravelly through ash,

the coalminer houses you lit; not fearing the ash
you breathed or these slither-fish, the thing that was
you; not fearing the race of cuts from razor-glass
or the nicotine-layers you made, the yellow
stains you became, they were the same; the reds
you turned to doorway cherries, the colours cut in
                                        your hands.

How fear came too late, then loss, the hands
that made glass moons, dripped ash,
held ice-creams. The sunrays still set in reds
in lines of northern doors. On Saturdays
you rested, though the ash did not: the yellow
stains, their shadows , cut you short, like broken glass.

Because of all this, the first poem I ever wrote was
for you – the killing ash, the first yellow – childhood
your hands made red-glow, magic glimpsed through glass.

Moments Musicaux

The new boiler
pumps through the arteries of the house
like the heart of a sleeping child

and below I hear my father
trellaa trill trelloo terrarrarra on the piano keys,
tiny silk-haired sorcerer
lifting the keys into song.

They rush and break into one another,
transform from lace to wind to white horse,
his fingers running where his eyes cannot see
into a medley of youth, his, mine

and I forgive the sharp edges
as they break into spray
the unsaid as it changes to falling pearls,
the early cold as it sifts away.

for the surgeon: when my dad was tiny

When my dad was tiny and white
and the hair dye ran out,
his legs stockinged,
slippered like an old lady's,
tubes dug in under sleeves,

you spoke to him as if you knew him big,

pacing round new cities in his checked hat,
memorising train timetables, weeding rose bushes,
building garden benches.

He clung to life
with every bran flake, meditation tape,
morning constitutional, cholesterol-free margarine
it took, to dig a smooth path to the heart,

studied his discomfort like a science
even in the well of it.

You spoke to him as if you knew all that.

When my dad was tiny
you spoke to him as if you knew him
big.

Violin romance

I knew from the first moment
we would find a voice, a way to sing,
you just wood and string
without me, I a reaching
in space, a breath between notes
without you.

      I knew how the singing
would be, like a kite on air,
a running like a wild child
into sea.

      I wonder now about the mystery
in your wood, if you mourn the forest
where you were, if the wine-brown memory
in your grain holds all the singing
we have done, all the ways we have
reached for new notes,
all the ways we have found our place.

Here is that song
*For Aleksander Wielhorski, my father's piano teacher,
Warsaw Conservatoire 1938*

I played your romance in the chapel
on a violin made of silk
and waited to hear what it told me,
what you wanted to say.

I think you wanted to say
there was always dance.

I think you wanted to say
that when there was no more water
you drank what you could of the sun,

when there was no more sun
you found the whites of the moon,

and when there was no more moon
you closed your eyes and sang.

I think you wanted to say:
Here is that song.

Oversteps Books Ltd

The Oversteps list includes books by the following poets:

David Grubb, Giles Goodland, Alex Smith, Will Daunt, Patricia Bishop, Christopher Cook, Jan Farquarson, Charles Hadfield, Mandy Pannett, Doris Hulme, James Cole, Helen Kitson, Bill Headdon, Avril Bruton, Marianne Larsen, Anne Lewis-Smith, Mary Maher, Genista Lewes, Miriam Darlington, Anne Born, Glen Phillips, Rebecca Gethin, W H Petty, Melanie Penycate, Andrew Nightingale, Caroline Carver, John Stuart, Rose Cook, Jenny Hope, Hilary Elfick, Jennie Osborne, Anne Stewart, Oz Hardwick, Angela Stoner, Terry Gifford, Michael Swan, Maggie Butt, Anthony Watts, Joan McGavin, Robert Stein, Graham High, Ross Cogan, Ann Kelley, A C Clarke, Diane Tang, Susan Taylor, R V Bailey, John Daniel, Alwyn Marriage, Simon Williams, Kathleen Kummer, Jean Atkin, Charles Bennett, Elisabeth Rowe, Marie Marshall, Ken Head, Robert Cole, Cora Greenhill, John Torrance, Michael Bayley, Christopher North, Simon Richey, Lynn Roberts, Sue Davies, Mark Totterdell, Michael Thomas, Ann Segrave, Helen Overell, Rose Flint, Denise Bennett, James Turner and Sue Boyle.

For details of all these books, information about Oversteps and up-to-date news, please look at our website and blog:

www.overstepsbooks.com
http://overstepsbooks.wordpress.com